this journal belongs to:

_____

_____

_____

this journal is dedicated to:

_____

_____

_____

The snow goose need not bathe to make
itself white. Neither need you do anything
but be yourself.

LAO TZU

Copyright © 2021 Theo Koffler
Published by
PESI Publishing
3839 White Ave
Eau Claire, WI 54703

Cover: Yellow.design & Amy Rubenzer
Developmental Editor: Elisse Gabriel
Copy Editor: Maria Sample
Layout: Yellow.design
ISBN: 9781683734239
All rights reserved.
Printed in Canada

Each purchase of *Life Notes* not only feels good, it also does good. Proceeds from this journal go directly toward supporting Mindfulness Without Borders, a nonprofit organization dedicated to providing mindfulness and social-emotional learning (SEL) programs to youth, educators, and health and corporate professionals in communities around the world. Available in English and Spanish, these evidence-based programs equip individuals with the essential life skills they need to bolster positive emotional development, critical thinking, resilience and overall well-being. With your support, we hope to reach more people so everyone can speak and truly listen to each other with a genuine understanding of our common humanity.

PESI Publishing
pesipublishing.com

life
notes
a guided journal

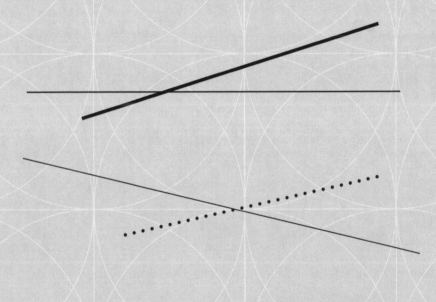

theo koffler

contents

foreword

Nothing is more powerful than an idea whose time has come.

VICTOR HUGO

Life Notes: A Guided Journal combines two well-tested contemplative techniques, the traditional Eastern meditative practice of mindfulness and the contemporary Western method of journaling, offering us a thoughtful and reflective way to bring awareness into our everyday lives. When awareness is present, we then have a real chance of bringing the best of our intentions, values, and aspirations into any situation, whether it's our relationship with ourselves or with others in our lives. No wonder the questions in this journal came from the distillation of wisdom and insights Theo Koffler personally gained from posing 88 questions to her parents as they were in the last decade of their lives. This guided journal provides a beautiful and practical framework to enter into a deep spiritual journey of self-examination that could lead to genuine mindfulness, opening ourselves to finding meaning and joy in our lives, based on embracing and celebrating our shared humanity.

THUPTEN JINPA, PhD, principal translator to H.H. the Dalai Lama and author of *A Fearless Heart: How the Courage to be Compassionate Can Transform Our Lives*

introduction

The idea for this journal came out of my love for connection.

As I witnessed my parents entering their last chapters of life, I realized there were so many questions I'd been longing for them to answer. So I began writing a list. Before I knew it, I'd written 88 questions. I inquired about my parents' ancestry, their values and beliefs, their achievements and challenges, and recorded these questions in two handcrafted books. When my parents' respective birthdays arrived, I presented each of them with my "Book of Questions." It was a gift with three remarkable outcomes. First, I'd received answers to long-held questions. Second, their books would become presents I would later pass on to my children, my siblings, and their children. And third, my parents' answers would create an invaluable link between them and future generations.

Watching my parents record their answers remains an unforgettable experience. My mother responded to the questions with abundant detail—a compelling blend of elegant poetic language and insight— while my father wrote short, pragmatic answers. Both books were filled with timeless wisdom and answers that further enriched my understanding of their journey. These handwritten journals became an instant treasure.

About a decade later, both my father and mother passed away after being together for nearly 70 years. Following their respective funerals, I made copies of these books for my siblings and their offspring as a way to memorialize my parents' spirits. As word spread, other family members and friends wanted copies too, making me realize the profound impact of capturing a loved one's stories. Therein lies the creation of this journal—a gift that truly keeps on giving.

The journal in your hands invites you to reflect upon the experiences that sum up your life thus far. After all, each person has a unique journey. We create, discover, and experience life differently. Think of this journal as a safe place to pull back the curtain and express your thoughts, emotions, moments, and memories.

If you want to take a deeper dive, consider sharing your journal with your loved ones so it weaves what is nearest to your heart into a larger tapestry, establishing deeper connections with those around you. After all, it is in the sharing of memories—of the people we've known, the experiences we've had, and the lives we've led—that we reveal our humanity and build bridges of understanding.

journaling tips

The key to answering these questions is to take your time. Part of the magic of this journal is to simply write what is true for you. In the process, you'll capture your memories and discover the power of having your experiences organized into neatly lined pages. Here are some helpful tips to keep in mind:

* keep the journal with you so you can write whenever inspiration strikes
* just before you write, follow the brief mindfulness practice at the beginning of each chapter to help you ground your attention in the moment
* answer the questions in any order you wish
* there are no right or wrong answers, just honest ones
* if a question is uncomfortable, acknowledge what arises without judgment
* if you don't have an answer to a question, simply move on to the next one
* revisit any unanswered questions when you are ready
* give yourself permission to write any length that feels comfortable for you
* set an intention with yourself to complete the journal
* make the experience enjoyable

breathe. reset. write.

At the beginning of each chapter, you'll find a brief mindfulness practice. Reflective practices like these are beneficial in refocusing your attention on your internal and external experiences in the moment. The intention is to notice your thoughts, feelings, and physical sensations— remembering that you are not pushing away your experiences, but accepting them just as they are with kindness and compassion. Simply, read and reflect upon each practice to help anchor your awareness in the moment, allowing you to pause from your daily routine, reset, and connect to the questions about your journey so far.

breathe. reset. write.

* sit in a comfortable position

* bring your attention to the flow of your breath coming into and
  leaving your body

* there's nothing special you need to do—your body knows how
  to breathe

* become aware of what you're feeling right now

* the idea is to let yourself feel what you're experiencing, without
  judgment

* as you sit still, continue to follow the natural flow of your breath

* if you notice your mind is distracted, know that it's normal

* simply redirect your attention back to the flow of your breath

* now rest in loving awareness that stillness grows in your heart as it
  becomes an intention in life

* allow each in-breath to be a new beginning and each out-breath to
  be a letting go

1
self

1

self

What is your favorite color?

BLUE

What sound do you find most soothing?

OCEAN / WATER

If you could live anywhere, where would it be?

IN DAVISON CONDO
PLACE with A Pool

What is the story behind your name?

Pure / Honest /

What three qualities define you?

Dependable

SHy

GOER

You are perfectly cast in your life.
I can't imagine anyone but you in the role.
Go play.

LIN-MANUEL MIRANDA

1
self

What was your favorite outdoor activity as a child?

SPORTS

Kickball

Baseball

Volley ball

What is your favorite pastime now?

MAKING PLANS - To Get OUT

What is a treasured memory from your childhood?

Waiting on my Dad To get off work @ 6:00Am sitting outside on the Curve / my mom would walk PAss my room / bed mAde-up Neat / Looking For Me!

When and where do you feel most at home?

AT my mother House

1
self

What is one of your shortcomings and how do you deal with it?

Getting hurt by Someone you Love
--- So I STAY AWAY

Ever tried. Ever failed. No matter.
Try again. Fail again. Fail better.

SAMUEL BECKETT

Describe something in nature that nourishes you.

Watching the Hummingbirds come to window
To feed

What is your favorite animal and why?

1
self

Which musician and song make you stand up and dance?

The Soul Generation Million Dollars
    PLus MORE!

What are your two favorite types of cuisine?

Bike Riding
Good EarthSenery

Describe one habit you would like to change and how it might impact you.

NoT moving my body ... Sitting to much ...
Need my own PLACE.

There is no passion to be found playing small—in settling for a life that is less than the one you are capable of living.

NELSON MANDELA

1

self

Share one thought that instantly brings a smile.

Someone thought of ME AND gave
me a present! UN Expectly

KINdNESS

What brings you strength?

KINdNESS

How do you describe your identity?

Sharing my Love / Kindness

First and foremost, we meet as human beings who
have so much in common: a heart, a face, a voice,
the presence of a soul, fears, hope, the ability to trust,
a capacity for compassion and understanding, the
kinship of being human.

RABBI ABRAHAM JOSHUA HESCHEL

1

self

What makes you sad?

Knowing
People that deliberate Hurt Someone
And is Sneeky + selfish/ Fonqy

What brings you happiness?

Sharing with Someone who has Less
Serving the Homeless { iN Need }

What are your fears?

STAYING SAD

If you could have three wishes, what would they be?

HAve
ConDo

BE A Blessing - to someone

serve + help Children / People Less Fortunate

breathe. reset. write.

* sit in a comfortable position

* bring your attention to the flow of your breath coming into and
  leaving your body

* take a moment to become aware of how your body feels

* now picture a beautiful mountain

* allow yourself to see its shape, from the base to the peak

* notice the mountain's size, texture, and solidity

* reflect on how a mountain changes with the weather—from the sun,
  wind, rain, and snow—yet it remains its essential self

* rest in loving awareness that stability grows in your heart as it
  becomes an intention in life

* bring your intention back to the flow of your breath

* allow each in-breath to be a new beginning and each out-breath
  to be a letting go

2
values

2
values

In what ways have you followed the footsteps of the people who raised you?

_____

_____

_____

_____

_____

_____

In what ways have you charted a new and different path?

_____

_____

_____

_____

_____

_____

_____

_____

_____

As a child, what did you want to be when you grew up?

_____

_____

_____

_____

_____

_____

_____

What is the most rebellious thing you did in your teenage years?

_____

_____

_____

_____

_____

_____

_____

_____

_____

_____

2
values

What advice do you give yourself when you are hurt by someone?

_____

_____

_____

_____

_____

_____

_____

_____

_____

_____

_____

_____

_____

_____

_____

_____

True forgiveness is when you can say,
"Thank you for that experience."

OPRAH WINFREY

Describe the impact a person from your childhood has had on the way you lead your life.

_____

_____

_____

_____

_____

_____

_____

_____

_____

_____

_____

_____

_____

_____

_____

_____

_____

2
values

Describe a time when you took a chance and learned something new about yourself.

_____

_____

_____

_____

_____

_____

Share a memory of a grandparent or elder who helped shape your values.

_____

_____

_____

_____

_____

_____

_____

What do you know now that you wish you'd understood when you were young?

_____

_____

_____

_____

_____

_____

_____

_____

_____

_____

_____

_____

The moment we decide to fulfill something,
we can do anything.

GRETA THUNBERG

2

values

Which of your values has changed over time and what influenced this shift?

If you could go back in time and say one thing to your former self, what moment would you return to and what would you say?

_____

_____

_____

_____

_____

_____

_____

_____

_____

_____

_____

One isn't necessarily born with courage, but one is born with potential. Without courage, we cannot practice any other virtue with consistency. We can't be kind, true, merciful, generous, or honest.

MAYA ANGELOU

2
values

Who is an influential person in your life today and how does this individual inspire you?

_____

_____

_____

_____

_____

_____

Share a quote, poem, or spiritual passage that moves you.

_____

_____

_____

_____

_____

_____

_____

_____

What is a family tradition or childhood event that helped shape
your life?

_____

_____

_____

_____

_____

_____

_____

What biases do you hold that you would like to change?

_____

_____

_____

_____

_____

_____

_____

_____

_____

2

values

Share three things you do when you want to brighten your day.

_____

_____

_____

_____

_____

_____

_____

_____

_____

_____

_____

So many of our dreams at first seem impossible,
then they seem improbable, and then,
when we summon the will,
they soon become inevitable.

CHRISTOPHER REEVE

Describe something you did when you were a teenager that
embarrassed you.

_____

_____

_____

_____

_____

_____

Describe an experience when you failed and what you learned.

_____

_____

_____

_____

_____

_____

_____

_____

_____

2

values

What are the chances or risks you can take to be the best
version of yourself?

_____

_____

_____

_____

_____

_____

_____

_____

_____

_____

_____

_____

_____

_____

What actions are you willing to take to make your community a better place?

breathe. reset. write.

* sit in a comfortable position

* bring your attention to the flow of your breath coming into and leaving your body

* take a moment to become aware of how your body feels

* call to mind one thing you value about yourself

* allow this attribute to expand in your heart

* notice how this makes you feel

* now focus on someone who has had a positive influence on your life

* allow this person's impact to root in your heart

* as you sit still, rest in loving awareness that appreciation grows in your heart as it becomes an intention in life

* bring your attention back to the flow of your breath

* allow each in-breath to be a new beginning and each out-breath to be a letting go

3
relationships

3
relationships

Where were your parents born?

_____

_____

_____

_____

If you could ask your mother one question, what would it be?

_____

_____

_____

_____

_____

If you could ask your father one question, what would it be?

_____

_____

_____

_____

_____

Is there anything you did or said to a parent or caregiver that you now regret?

3

relationships

What advice did a grandparent or mentor give you that is relevant to you today?

_____

_____

_____

_____

_____

_____

_____

_____

_____

_____

_____

_____

_____

Listen to the ancestors, to spirit, to the trees, to
the animals. Focus on ritual. Listen to all those forces
that come and speak to us that we usually ignore.

SOBONFU SOMÉ

Describe what you find most interesting about your best friend.

_____

_____

_____

_____

_____

_____

Share the names of two long-term friends and how they have
influenced you.

_____

_____

_____

_____

_____

_____

_____

_____

3
relationships

Is there a relationship in your past you wish had been different? Why?

Describe a time you were pleasantly surprised by an unforeseen change in someone else.

_____

_____

_____

_____

_____

_____

_____

_____

_____

_____

_____

_____

_____

_____

_____

_____

_____

3
relationships

How has your suffering shaped your relationships?

_____

_____

_____

_____

_____

_____

_____

_____

_____

_____

_____

_____

_____

_____

_____

_____

If you can't love yourself, how in the hell
are you gonna love somebody else?

RUPAUL

How do you express your appreciation for others?

_____

_____

_____

_____

_____

_____

_____

_____

What is something a parent or caregiver did or said that upset you at the time, but you now understand?

_____

_____

_____

_____

_____

_____

_____

_____

_____

3
relationships

How do the masks you wear affect the way in which you connect with others?

_____

_____

_____

_____

_____

_____

Have you ever avoided confronting something in yourself you wish you could reveal to others?

_____

_____

_____

_____

_____

_____

_____

_____

Have you ever done something to gain approval and later regretted it?

_____

_____

_____

_____

_____

_____

_____

_____

_____

_____

_____

_____

_____

_____

Let us be grateful to people who make us happy;
they are the charming gardeners who make
our souls blossom.

MARCEL PROUST

3
relationships

What is an assumption someone made about you that was wrong?

_____

_____

_____

_____

_____

_____

_____

What is an assumption you made about someone that was wrong?

_____

_____

_____

_____

_____

_____

_____

_____

_____

Share the story of a time when you did something for someone that made a positive impact.

3

relationships

If you could offer three pieces of advice about relationships to future generations, what would they be?

If you decided to write a letter to the political leader of your country, what would your message say?

breathe. reset. write. ♡MAC

Listen to the sounds of nature.

* sit in a comfortable position

* bring your attention to the flow of your breath coming into and leaving your body

* take a moment to become aware of how your body feels

* now call to mind someone for whom you feel grateful

* notice how you feel when you think of this person

* allow your appreciation for this person to root in your heart

* notice how your body feels

* as you sit still, rest in loving awareness that gratitude grows in your heart as it becomes an intention in life

* bring your attention back to the flow of your breath

* allow each in-breath to be a new beginning and each out-breath to be a letting go

4
gratitude

4
gratitude

Write a list of five things for which you are grateful.

_____

_____

_____

_____

_____

Name someone for whom you are grateful and describe how this person has enriched your life.

_____

_____

_____

_____

_____

What are you grateful for about yourself?

_____

_____

_____

_____

_____

Share one experience that helped you grow.

It's a funny thing about life, once you begin to take note of the things you are grateful for, you begin to lose sight of the things that you lack.

GERMANY KENT

4
gratitude

Describe a situation in which the impact of your kindness surprised you.

_____

_____

_____

_____

_____

_____

_____

What makes you feel grateful about the place where you live?

_____

_____

_____

_____

_____

_____

_____

_____

_____

Share one challenge you've faced for which you are grateful.

_____

_____

_____

_____

_____

_____

_____

What do you do to take care of your environment?

_____

_____

_____

_____

_____

_____

_____

_____

_____

4
gratitude

Describe a time when someone helped make sense of a challenge you were facing. What did you learn?

_____

_____

_____

_____

_____

_____

_____

_____

_____

_____

_____

_____

_____

We hold the key to lasting happiness in our own hands.
For it is not joy that makes us grateful;
it is gratitude that makes us joyful.

BROTHER DAVID STEINDL-RAST

If you could express gratitude toward someone, what would you say and to whom?

_____

_____

_____

_____

_____

_____

Name one act of kindness that had a ripple effect you could never have predicted.

_____

_____

_____

_____

_____

_____

_____

_____

4
gratitude

What does compassion mean to you?

_____

_____

_____

_____

_____

_____

_____

What is more challenging, being compassionate to yourself or
to others, and why?

_____

_____

_____

_____

_____

_____

_____

_____

What does it mean to live a life of gratitude, and are you living it?

4
gratitude

In what ways can you be of service to others?

_____

_____

_____

_____

_____

_____

_____

_____

_____

_____

_____

_____

Appreciate how rare and full of potential
your situation is in this world, then take joy
in it, and use it to your best advantage.

THE 14th DALAI LAMA

List three things you take for granted and share a way you can express your gratitude for each one.

4

gratitude

What can you do to make another person's life marginally better at this very moment?

_____

_____

_____

_____

_____

_____

_____

Describe a time when you were kind to a stranger and how this experience affected you.

_____

_____

_____

_____

_____

_____

_____

_____

_____

If you had one year left to live, what would you most like to do?

breathe. reset. write.

- sit in a comfortable position
- allow your breath to steady your awareness in the present moment
- now call to mind an image of a lake
- picture its shape, size, and natural surroundings
- consider how the surface of the lake experiences continuous changes
- yet the bottom of the lake remains relatively still
- imagine yourself finding the same stillness when emotions are stirred up within you
- notice how this makes you feel
- as you sit still, rest in loving awareness that inner peace grows in your heart as it becomes an intention in life
- bring your attention back to the flow of your breath
- allow each in-breath to be a new beginning and each out-breath to be a letting go

5
choices

5
choices

What was your first job?

_____

_____

_____

_____

_____

What is the best decision you ever made?

_____

_____

_____

_____

What is the hardest decision you ever made?

_____

_____

_____

_____

_____

Describe your greatest disappointment or struggle in life.

_____

_____

_____

_____

_____

_____

_____

_____

_____

_____

_____

_____

_____

_____

_____

Not everything that is faced can be changed,
but nothing can be changed until it is faced.

JAMES BALDWIN

5

choices

What is a thought that wakes you up in the middle of the night?

_____

_____

_____

_____

_____

_____

If you could pass on one piece of advice to younger generations about making good decisions, what would it be?

_____

_____

_____

_____

_____

_____

_____

What has been your most powerful conviction so far?

_____

_____

_____

_____

_____

_____

_____

_____

_____

_____

_____

_____

_____

_____

_____

_____

5

choices

If you could volunteer your time right now, what would you choose to do?

_____

_____

_____

_____

_____

_____

_____

_____

_____

_____

_____

Someone is sitting in the shade today because
someone planted a tree a long time ago.

WARREN BUFFETT

What accomplishment makes you feel most proud? Describe how this achievement shaped you.

5

choices

What character traits have helped you reach your goals?

_____

_____

_____

_____

_____

_____

_____

What is/was your career and what led you to this line of work?

_____

_____

_____

_____

_____

_____

_____

_____

_____

_____

Describe an experience when you were persistent and how it helped you accomplish something important.

5
choices

How willing are you to listen to viewpoints with which you disagree?

_____

_____

_____

_____

_____

_____

What's one thing you do every day that helps sustain our planet?

_____

_____

_____

_____

_____

_____

_____

_____

Which decisions did you make in the past that you regret or wish you could change?

_____

_____

_____

_____

_____

_____

_____

_____

_____

_____

_____

_____

_____

_____

_____

_____

5
choices

What is something in your environment you are inspired to protect?

_____

_____

_____

_____

_____

_____

What is one thing you've always desired and still do not have?

_____

_____

_____

_____

_____

_____

_____

_____

If you could write a note to a friend who helped you make an important decision, what would it say?

_____

_____

_____

_____

_____

_____

_____

_____

_____

_____

_____

_____

_____

It is not our differences that divide us. It is
our inability to recognize, accept, and celebrate
those differences.

AUDRE LORDE

5

choices

Share a story of a time you had a sudden change of mind that had a life-altering effect.

_____

_____

_____

_____

_____

_____

_____

_____

_____

_____

_____

_____

_____

_____

_____

_____

Where would you like to see yourself in ten years?

The world does not deliver meaning to you.
You have to make it meaningful... and decide
what you want and need and must do.

ZADIE SMITH

breathe. reset. write.

* sit in a comfortable position

* take a moment to become aware of how your body feels

* allow your breath to steady your awareness in the present moment

* begin sending yourself wishes for happiness, good health, and peace

* silently repeat to yourself, "may I be happy, may I be healthy, may I be at peace"

* notice how this makes you feel

* now picture someone dear to you and send wishes for that person's happiness, good health, and peace

* notice how this makes you feel

* as you sit still, rest in loving awareness that compassion grows in your heart as it becomes an intention in life

* bring your attention back to the flow of your breath

* allow each in-breath to be a new beginning and each out-breath to be a letting go

6
insights

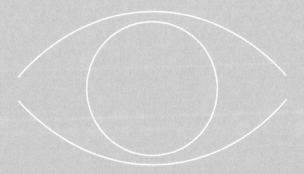

6

insights

If you could go back and relive one specific time in your life, when would it be and why?

_____

_____

_____

_____

_____

_____

If you knew you couldn't fail, what would you do?

_____

_____

_____

_____

_____

_____

_____

_____

_____

What brings meaning to your life right now?

_____

_____

_____

_____

_____

_____

_____

What is your least favorite memory?

_____

_____

_____

_____

_____

Owning our story can be hard but not nearly as difficult as spending our lives running from it.

BRENÉ BROWN

6

insights

If you could write a message to yourself and read it in five years, what would it say?

_____

_____

_____

_____

_____

_____

_____

_____

_____

_____

_____

_____

I think everyone makes a mistake at least once in their life.
The important thing is what you learn from it.

MALALA YOUSAFZAI

How do you manage uncertainty in your life?

_____

_____

_____

_____

_____

_____

_____

What is the difference between how you feel about yourself now and
how you felt about yourself when you were younger?

_____

_____

_____

_____

_____

_____

_____

_____

6

insights

Which historical figures are a source of inspiration or motivation?

_____

_____

_____

_____

_____

_____

_____

What qualities do you embrace to stay focused on your ideals?

_____

_____

_____

_____

_____

_____

_____

_____

_____

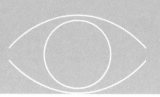

What significant world events have occurred during your life that have changed your perspective?

_____

_____

_____

_____

_____

_____

_____

_____

_____

_____

_____

_____

_____

_____

_____

6
insights

How has your current mindset changed from previous decades?

_____

_____

_____

_____

_____

_____

_____

_____

_____

_____

_____

_____

_____

_____

_____

_____

_____

How do you feel about getting older?

_____

_____

_____

_____

_____

_____

_____

_____

_____

_____

_____

_____

_____

Every day will bring the experience of newness and
creativity—if you allow happiness to unfold.

DEEPAK CHOPRA

6
insights

If you could travel anywhere in the world, where would you go?

_____

_____

_____

_____

_____

What aspects of your life have surprised you?

_____

_____

_____

_____

_____

What role does love or intimacy play in your life?

_____

_____

_____

_____

_____

If you could look into a crystal ball and learn something about the future, what would you like to know?

_____

_____

_____

_____

_____

_____

_____

_____

_____

_____

_____

Fight for the things that you care about, but do it in a way that will lead others to join you.

RUTH BADER GINSBERG

6
insights

Describe an embarrassing moment in your adult life.

_____

_____

_____

_____

_____

_____

_____

_____

_____

_____

_____

_____

_____

_____

_____

_____

_____

_____

If you could come back as something in your next life, what or who would it be?

_____

_____

_____

_____

_____

_____

_____

_____

_____

_____

_____

_____

_____

_____

_____

_____

_____

6

insights

What in life doesn't make sense to you?

_____

_____

_____

_____

_____

_____

_____

_____

_____

_____

_____

_____

_____

_____

_____

_____

_____

_____

What do you think the world needs more of, right now?

_____

_____

_____

_____

_____

_____

_____

_____

_____

_____

_____

_____

_____

_____

_____

_____

And the day came when the risk to remain tight in a bud was
more painful than the risk it took to blossom.

ELIZABETH APPELL

6
insights

Describe your experience in completing this journal.

_____

_____

_____

_____

_____

_____

_____

_____

_____

_____

_____

_____

_____

_____

_____

_____

_____

_____

_____

_____

_____

_____

One day I will be an ancestor and I want my descendants to know that I used my voice so that they could have a future.

AUTUMN PELTIER

congratulations, you've finished!

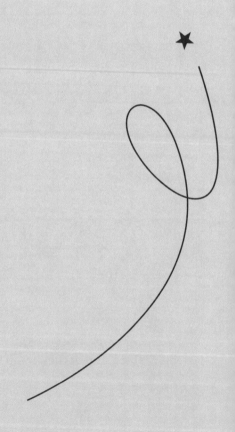

The only limit to the height of your achievements is the reach of your dreams and your willingness to work for them.

MICHELLE OBAMA

acknowledgments

I am forever grateful to my parents, Murray and Marvelle Koffler. Their focus on humanity led me to the important discovery that a meaningful life is inextricably connected to one's purpose, an affinity to do good and indefatigable kindness. I am wholeheartedly indebted to so many people. To my children, Omri and Itamar, for being my teachers and for shaping the person I have become. To my cherished family and longtime friends, for their constant companionship and for changing my life for the better. To my dear colleagues, whose friendship, maverick thinking and innovations continue to open new windows of understanding. To Susan and Marcus Hewitt, for their discerning attention to design. To Elisse Gabriel and Maria Sample, for their careful editing of the written word. To Karsyn Morse, Acquisitions Editor at PESI Publishing, who believed in this journal of questions. And to Thupten Jinpa, who wrote the dedication for this journal. His extraordinary service as principal translator to His Holiness the Dalai Lama has demonstrated that dialogue and compassion are the paths to an interconnected world.

about the author

Born in Toronto, Theo Koffler was the cofounder and VP of Super-Pharm Israel Ltd., one of Israel's largest pharmacy chains. When a personal health crisis prompted a change of focus, she pivoted from her corporate career to explore the role of social-emotional intelligence and mindfulness on individual and societal well-being. Theo then founded Mindfulness Without Borders (MWB), a nonprofit organization that advances mindfulness-based learning programs in educational, healthcare and corporate settings.

A mother, philanthropist, public speaker and advocate for mental health, Theo leads MWB educational workshops and training sessions around the world. When not working on her initiatives, she mentors young entrepreneurs, relaxes with her sons, enjoys entertaining family and friends, and spends time in nature to nurture her well-being.